Cats
Out of the Bag

Cats
Out of the Bag

401 Purr-fectly Pleasing
Tidbits for Cat Lovers

Compiled by Terry, Don and Ken Beck

PREMIUM PRESS AMERICA
NASHVILLE, TENNESSEE

CATS OUT OF THE BAG

Published by PREMIUM PRESS AMERICA

Copyright © 1996 by Terry, Don, and Ken Beck

ISBN 1-887654-16-X

Library of Congress Catalog Card Number 96-69012

PREMIUM PRESS AMERICA gift books are available at special discounts for premiums, sales promotions, fund-raising, or educational use. For details contact the Publisher at P.O. Box 159015, Nashville, TN 37215, or phone toll free (800) 891-7323 or (615)256-8484, or fax us at (615)256-8624.

For more information visit our web site at *www.premiumpress.com.*

Cover design and layout by Brent Baldwin
Cover art copyright Totem Graphics and the Corel Corporation

First Edition July 1996
2 3 4 5 6 7 8 9 10

Dedication

To all the veterinarians who not only love and care for our cats, but believe us when we say they're human.

INTRODUCTION
By Sam the Cat

The clowder elected me to introduce this small volume of feline facts for your fun and fancy. I guess because I happen to be polydactyl they thought I could do the best job. Anyway, whether you're a true ailurophile or just a distant admirer, we think you'll enjoy this book. Now don't read ahead. Remember, curiosity killed the cat.

I don't think that I'd be letting the cat out of the bag if I told you that we felines are now the No. 1 pet in America. Whether purebred or a moggie, you'll find us all friendly and true. We've been involved with man since history was first recorded, and we've been worshipped and persecuted; thought to be good luck and bad. We've lived like kings and we've lived like beggars. After all is said and done, we just want a good home and a caring owner. In return, you'll have our everlasting affection.

Now read on and you'll find that we're all digitigrade and most of us are crepuscular. We definitely don't want an onyxectomy and even though we're said to have nine lives, we'd prefer you not to think of ways to skin us.

You'll learn that we're well acquainted with Hollywood and at home in the White House. We've saved the world from pestilence and disease. And we've inspired many a writer, artist, poet and cartoonist.

Well, enough of my caterwauling. Enjoy this book, then give a cat a home if you've not already done so. We'll sure love you for it.

For my feline friends,
Sam the Cat

Cats Out of the Bag

1. Cats have lived with humans for about 4,000 years. But they still won't come when you call them.

2. In the U.S. there are 64 million cats which live in 32 percent of American homes. The cat is now the Number 1 pet in America. And you thought this country was going to the dogs.

3. When a domestic cat goes after mice, about one pounce in three results in a catch. Hey, a .333 batting average is nothing to sneeze at.

4. The cat lover is an ailurophile, while a cat hater is an ailurophobe. Among the world's greatest cat haters were Genghis Khan, Alexander the Great, Julius Caesar, Napoleon and Hitler. Definitely bad company.

 **Cats Out of the Bag**

5. *The London Times* recorded in 1950 that a young cat, the pet of the cook of the nearby Hotel Belvedere, climbed the Matterhorn in the Alps behind a group of mountaineers. The climbers brought the cat down and gave it a good supper. It was then named Cervinis, the Italian word for Matterhorn.

6. A cat named Towser eliminated 28,899 mice while he was employed by the Glenturret distillery near Crieff, Tayside, England, a cat world record. He retired at the ripe old age of 24. Reckon he hated meeses to pieces.

7. The first cat museum open to the public was Katzenmuseum in Riehen, Switzerland, on June 12, 1982. There are now two more: the Musee du Chat in Ainvelle, France, and the Kattenkabinet in Amsterdam, Holland.

Cats Out of the Bag

8. The first official cat show in Great Britain was an exhibition at London's Crystal Palace in July 1871. Organized by Harrison Weir, lots of people and 160 cool cats showed up to compete for $100 in prize money. How many ducats is that?

9. The Egyptians were the first humans to tame the cat. The Kaffir or Cape cat, *Felis libica*, is believed to be the wild ancestor of the domestic cat.

10. One summer night in 1955 in Keston, England, Winifred Mansell's pet cat Ginny came limping home. Mrs. Mansell removed what she thought to be glass from Ginny's left front foot. The glass proved to be two diamonds worth around $600 apiece. Hmmm, could Ginny have been a cat burglar?

11. Felix the Cat sprang to life in 1919 and was the first animated cartoon character to go on to star in a newspaper comic strip. His name was spun off the word felicity which means great happiness. By 1922 he was the lucky mascot of the New York Yankees, and when Charles Lindbergh made his famous solo flight across the Atlantic in 1927, a Felix doll accompanied him.

12. As I Was Going to St. Ives,
I met a man with seven wives,
Each wife had seven sacks,
Each sack had seven cats,
Each cat had seven kits,
Kits, cats, sacks and wives,
How many cats were going to St. Ives?
Answer: None, but there were 2,401 cats and kits in the wives' sacks.

Cats Out of the Bag

13. The first cats to occupy the White House belonged to Willy Lincoln, Abe's son.

14. Ernest Hemingway had many cats as pets, and today visitors may see their descendants and visit the old cats by the sea at the Hemingway museum in Key West, Florida. For him, the cat bell tolls.

15. Cat stamps were officially issued by the United States Post Office on February 5, 1988, with four stamps with two cats on each stamp. These mail cats included: Maine Coon/Burmese, American Shorthair/Persian, Siamese/Exotic Shorthair and Abyssinian/Himalayan.

16. Singapura are the smallest cats, averaging from four to six pounds.

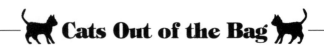 **Cats Out of the Bag**

17. The top 10 favorite breeds of American cats, according to the Cat Fancier's Association (1993) are: (in order) Persian, Maine Coon, Siamese, Abyssinian, Exotic, Scottish Fold, Oriental Shorthair, American Shorthair, Burmese and Birman.

18. A survey done in 1988 by a cat magazine asked readers to pick words to describe cats; the No. 1 choice was affectionate, listed by 95% of the readers.

19. The only live animal allowed in ancient Roman temples was the cat.

20. The oldest known cat to have kittens was Kitty, who gave birth to twins in 1987 at the age of 30. They were her 217th and 218th kits.

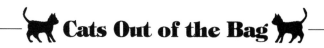

Cats Out of the Bag

21. The Japanese island Irimote is home to the rarest feline, the Irimote. There are only about 80 of these nocturnal cats left. These cats, discovered in 1967, are the size of a domestic cat and are protected by law.

22. "If man could be crossed with the cat, it would improve man, but would deteriorate the cat."
— Mark Twain

23. The word for "cat" in most languages appears to trace back to North Africa where "quttah" is the oldest known form of the word.

24. The offspring of a male lion and a female tiger is called a liger, while the offspring of a male tiger and a female lion is called a tiglon. We're not lion.

Cats Out of the Bag

25. Chicago's Tree House is a facility for abandoned or injured felines. The shelter, which opened in 1971 and has treated thousands of cats, is located in an old Victorian house.

26. The word "cat" first appeared in literature in the works of Palladius around 400 A.D.

27. Kitty Litter was invented in 1947 when delivery man Edward Lowe, who was out of sand, suggested to a cat owner that she use a grease and oil absorbent instead. Today cat box filler is an $800 million industry as about 1.8 million tons of cat litter are sold annually.

28. In 1970, the Isle of Man issued a one-crown coin with Queen Elizabeth II on one side and a Manx cat on the other, making it reportedly the only coin in the world with a cat on it.

Cats Out of the Bag

29. A group of cats, when not a litter, is called a clowder. A group of such kittens is called a kyndyl.

30. The highest percentage of cats with the extra-toes syndrome has been reported in the Boston area, where about 12 percent of the cats may have five toes with one of them enlarged or six or seven toes on either the front or back feet.

31. In 1961, rats were overrunning the rice fields of Borneo to such a degree that the stray cats of Singapore were captured and parachuted from planes into the rice fields and thus saved the crops. Sounds like it was raining cats to me.

32. Cat saliva contains a deodorizing agent which keeps it clean and healthy. Talk about a good licking.

33. The Cheshire Cat in Lewis Carroll's *Alice in Wonderland* vanishes, beginning with the end of the tail, until only the grin remains.
"Well! I've often seen a cat without a grin," thought Alice: "but a grin without a cat! It's the most curious thing I ever saw in my life!"
Alice also had her own cat named Dinah.

34. Cartoonist Jim Davis' Garfield the cat was voiced by Lorenzo Music, the same voice behind Carlton the doorman on *The Mary Tyler Moore Show*. The Garfield comic strip began in 1978. He's been loving lasagna ever since.

35. The term "cat's pajamas" comes from E.B. Katz, an English tailor of the late 1700s and early 1800s, who made the finest silk pajamas for royalty and other wealthy patrons. Nothing like a cat nap in Katz' pj's.

Cats Out of the Bag

36. A sleeping kitten drawn by Austrian artist Guido Gruenwald was selected as the symbol for the Chesapeake and Ohio Railroad in 1934. "Chessie" has since appeared on millions of calendars and quite a few boxcars.

37. The average weight of a female cat is 7.2 pounds; for a male cat, 8.6 pounds.

38. An anatomical curiosity of white cats is that if they have blue eyes, they probably cannot hear.

39. Some cats can smell the oil in catnip when its ratio to air is as low as one part per billion. I'll be doggone.

40. Cats and dogs are about equally intelligent, and cats can be trained as easily as dogs. Heel, Morris.

Cats Out of the Bag

41. With the single exception of lions, wild cats become solitary animals after they leave their mothers and siblings. Lions live in groups numbering from four to 30. They've got a lot of pride.

42. More than 300,000 cat mummies were found in one Egyptian temple in 1850. Twenty tons of the mummies were shipped to Liverpool, England, where they were sold at $18 a ton for fertilizer. The auctioneer used an embalmed cat for his gavel. That was one going, going, gone cat.

43. The name of the M-G-M lion shown roaring at the beginning of their black and white films was named Slats. Once color technology came along, M-G-M hired a new lion named Tanner to fill the bill.

44. Cat puberty begins at about four months of age. Those young whiskersnappers.

45. MGM's Tom and Jerry copped seven Academy Awards. Their first cartoon, *Puss Gets the Boot*, was seen in 1940. Their names were selected via a contest among studio employees. Both also appeared with Esther Williams in her 1953 flick *Dangerous When Wet*. Notice the cat got top billing.

46. Vanna White's pair of cats are named Ashley and Rhett. They are wheely FORTUNatE cats.

47. Charles Dickens had a cat named William but after he had kittens, his name was changed to Wilhelmina. The cat had a habit of snuffing out Dickens' reading candle with her paw. Ah, a tale of one kitty.

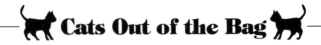

Cats Out of the Bag

48. The word cat in other languages: kocka in Czech, kat in Dutch, chat in French, katze in German, popoki in Hawaiian, chatul in Hebrew, gatto in Italian, neko in Japanese, koshka in Russian, gato in Spanish and paka in Swahili.

49. The American Cat Association is the first and oldest registry in North America. Its roots began in 1897 with the formation of the Beresford Cat Club in Chicago. In 1904 some members of the Beresford Club began the American Cat Association.

50. Englishman Leoni Clarke performed with a troupe of 50 trained cats which among other tricks, would step over arrangements of mice, canaries and rats, as well as jump through fiery hoops and parachute down from the ceiling. Clarke called himself "The King of the Cats."

51. The jaguar is the largest North American cat, followed by the puma, which can leap 20 feet in one jump. Jumpin' Jehosocat!

52. There are 38 species of the cat family, including 31 species of *Felis*, six species of *Panthera*, and one of *Acinonyx*.

53. Cats traditionally dislike water but bobcats, ocelots and jaguars do swim, and of domestic cats, only the Van cat of Turkey enjoys taking a dip.

54. The puddy cat Tweety Bird always tawt he taw was Sylvester, who first appeared in 1945. He didn't pair with Tweety until 1947 in *Tweetie Pie*, which won an Oscar for best short subject. Sylvester's voice came from the late great Mel Blanc. Sufferin' succotash.

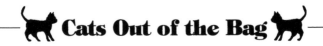 **Cats Out of the Bag**

55. Morris the Cat, the commercial cat for 9-Lives catfood, was a contender for President in 1986. He ran as a Democat. Morris made his first commercial in 1969, at the same time his name was changed from Lucky. He was discovered at the Hinsdale Humane Society Shelter near Chicago. Over a period of 10 years he made forty commercials and one movie, *Shamus*. The finicky feline died at age 17 in 1978.

56. The King of Wales, Howell the Good, passed the first British law dealing with cat crimes in about A.D. 945. Any person who mistreated, stole or killed a cat was to be fined one sheep along with its lambs. He also placed a value on cats: a kitten would be worth two cents once it opened its eyes and worth four cents after it had killed its first mouse.

 **Cats Out of the Bag**

57. Known as the "Cat Raphael," Swiss painter Gottfried Mind only did portraits of the cats of the French aristocracy. He painted a pretty kitty.

58. At least one cat helped in the building of Grand Coulee Dam in 1930 as a string was tied to its tail and it walked through drainpipes, connecting ropes to cables.

59. Pluto is *The Black Cat* in Edgar Allen Poe's eerie short story about a cat's vengeance upon an evil drunkard. In the weeks before Poe's wife Virginia died, his cat, Catarina, kept her warm by lying on her.

60. Cats are native to five continents but not to Australia or Antarctica. Today, only Antarctica remains catless.

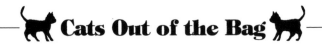

Cats Out of the Bag

61. Even though half of Europe was wiped out by the Black Plague of the 1300s, cats and their rat-catching abilities helped save thousands by wiping out the disease-carrying rodents.

62. The people of Paraguay employ their cats on search and destroy missions for rattlesnakes.

63. Somewhat like a monkey in the way it runs sideways and even holds its food, the Somali breed looks remarkably like a fox. Quiet cats, they love people, hiding in secret places and playing with water.

64. Arnold Schwarzenegger's mother, Aurelia, rescues stray cats (and dogs) while she serves as honorary president of Noah's Ark House in her hometown, Graz, Austria. She is a true Aurelia-phile.

Cats Out of the Bag

65. The Pink Panther was first seen during the credits of Blake Edwards' *Pink Panther* film. In 1964 he appeared in his first cartoon, *The Pink Phink*. He, voiced by Paul Frees, only spoke in two cartoons, *Sink Pink* (1965) and *Super Pink* (1966). What he said: "Why can't man be more like animals?"

66. The most popular names for tom cats in the United States, according to *Cat Fancy*, are Charlie, Max, Mickey, Rocky, Sam, Sammy, Smokey, Tiger and Toby. For female cats the top names are Fluffy, Missy, Misty, Muffin, Patches, Pumpkin, Samantha, Tabitha and Tigger. An in Great Britain the Top 10 most popular names, according to the British Market Research Bureau, are (from No. 1 to No. 10) Sooty, Smokie, Brandy, Fluffy, Tiger, Tibbie, Tiggie, Tom, Kitty and Sam.

Cats Out of the Bag

67. In 1993, Kingston, Canada, residents Jack and Donna Wright had about 640 pet cats living in their house. Sounds like a cat-astrophe.

68. Sir Isaac Newton must have been a feline fancier as he is credited with inventing the cat-flap to allow his cat free access to his house. Then there was the time his cat fell out of a tree.

69. In a famous ancient fight, the Romans took cats with them into battle against the Egyptians knowing of their love for cats, and the Egyptians preferred to give up the city of Pelusa rather than risk hurting a feline.

70. That spooky glow of a cat's eye at night in bright light is called night shine. It is a reflection of the cat's retina, which is visible because the pupil was opened wide just before the light hit it.

Cats Out of the Bag

71. Within two to three days after birth, each kitten in a litter chooses his own teat, and from then on uses only that one.

72. America's first cat exhibition was in Madison Square Garden from May 8-11, 1895. Over 200 cats were shown in cages.

73. The basic colors of cats are tabby, black, orange, tortoiseshell (calico), white, and siamese.

74. A blind cat with whiskers can walk without bumping into objects. There has been at least one cat that served as a seeing-eye cat for a human in the U.S.

75. Approximately 50 percent of all cats are right-handed. The other half are southpaws, of course.

Cats Out of the Bag

76. One of our favorite cats, the tiger, has declined from around one million at the turn of the century to about 7,000, with three of the eight varieties now extinct, a sad but true tiger tale.

77. On August 7, 1970, a Burmese cat named Tarawood Antigone gave birth to the largest domestic cat litter when she birthed 19 kittens in England. Free kittens anyone.

78. The jewel cat's-eye is a chrysoberyl stone, cut into an oval, that has a light line in it that changes shape as the gem is moved, making it look like a cat's eye.

79. There was once a firehouse cat in Long Beach, California, that was the first one to slide down the pole when the bells began to ring.

80. *The Aristocats* (1970) was the Disney Studio's first animated feature to be produced without Walt Disney. It was about a mother cat, Duchess (voiced by Eva Gabor), and her three kittens who are abandoned in the French countryside and must find their way back to Paris.

81. The Abyssinian is the most feral in appearance and is also known as the cat from the Blue Nile. Its voice is described as bell-like. The first Abyssinian to enter England was Zula in 1868. The breed reached the U.S. in 1909.

82. The third-highest grossing film in Japanese movie history is *The Adventures of Chatran* and is about a farm cat and his adventures with the other farm animals. In 1987 it was the Number 1 film of the year and became a national cult.

Cats Out of the Bag

83. Charles Lindbergh's cat Patsy was the first domestic cat to be on an official government stamp when Spain released a series of stamps in honor of famous aviators in 1930. Guess that had Patsy flying high. The first wild cat on a stamp was a Malayan tiger issued in 1891.

84. Cats, in the tradition of Morris, rarely eat crumbs.

85. Bast, or Bastet, was the ancient Egyptian cat goddess of love and fertility and had the body of a woman with the head of a cat.

86. Kittens are born blue-eyed. If their eyes change colors, it generally occurs at four to five weeks of age.

87. The gestation period of the cat is 61 to 65 days and a litter can have more than one father.

Cats Out of the Bag

88. According to Huck Finn, a dead cat taken to the fresh grave of a wicked person at midnight was a sure cure for warts. The devil that came for the deceased would be followed by the cat and the warts.

89. New York's Catskill Mountains were named after the bobcat by Henry Hudson. Kaatskill means wildcat creek.

90. During a four-week period in 1938, Peter, a five-month-old kitten, killed 400 rats in an English railway station. He was "on track" when it came to rats.

91. The Maneki Neko, or Beckoning Cat, is a Japanese good-luck symbol. Small statues of this tricolor cat are found in the windows of many shops and eating places to invite in customers.

Cats Out of the Bag

92. Cats, of all domestic animals, probably pose the least risk to the health of human beings.

93. The cat is the only animal that purrs. Domestic cats can purr while inhaling or exhaling, while the big cats, like lions and tigers, may only purr while exhaling.

94. A London cat was reported to have survived a 120-foot fall after jumping from an eleven-story apartment window. One life down, eight to go.

95. "Mongrel," though usually thought of in canine terms, is also the correct term for a nonpedigreed cat, however, in England most cat owners prefer to use the word "moggie."

96. Of homes that have pets, 42 percent have two or more cats. Double your pleasure.

97. Barring injury or accident, most domestic cats will live between nine to 15 years. The longest recorded lifespan of a feline is 36 years by an English tabby named "Puss" who died in 1939. In his old age he was said to have been a crabby tabby.

98. Cat Tail Tells Tale: Curved down and then up at the tip means relaxed; Slightly raised and curved - mild curiosity; Erect with tip also vertical - greeting; Fully lowered, tucked between legs - submissive; Swishing from side to side - angry; Lowered, fluffed out - fearful; Still with twitching tip - irritated but not angry; Straight and fully bristled - aggressive; Arched and bristled - defensive.

99. Practically all tortoiseshell cats are female.

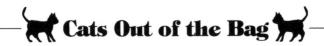

Cats Out of the Bag

100. The name of the operation where a cat is declawed is called an onyxectomy. Declawing your cat is illegal in the United Kingdom.

101. "Ah! cats are a mysterious kind of folk." — Sir Walter Scott

102. In Aesop's *The Fox and the Cat*, the cat outsmarts the wily, bragging fox by using his one way to escape from the hounds, while the fox is caught while trying to decide which of his 100 escape plans to use.

103. A cat can turn its outer ear toward a sound about 10 times faster than a dog. A cat's ears are a lot more sensitive than human ears. A cat can hear sounds up to two octaves higher than the highest note a human can.

104. The American Curl was discovered in 1981 in Lakewood, California, as a stray black female kitten, Shulamith. Her first litter of four kittens produced two more with curly ears, which were determined to be a result of a dominant gene. All true American Curls are ancestors of Shulamith, which at birth have straight ears which start turning back at two to 10 days.

105. The maximum speed of a domestic cat is 30 miles per hour, making him faster than the elephant, pig, black mamba snake, squirrel, and you.

106. Guffey, Colorado, population 35, elected a cat, Wiffy La Gone, as mayor in 1990. The cat has since been hounded out of office by a golden retriever named Shanda.

Cats Out of the Bag

107. If your cat's temperature exceeds 103 degrees, call your veterinarian.

108. What to do when your cat won't use the litter box? Try *How To Toilet Train Your Cat* by Paul Kunkel.

109. Gunther Gebel-Williams is truly "Lord of the Ring." During his long-running career with Barnum & Bailey and Ringling Brothers Circus, he and his big cats put on more than 10,000 performances.

110. The first English book about cat care was written by Lady Crust in 1856 and was 31 pages long. A more exhaustive volume came along in 1874 with William Gordon Stable's 500-page-long *Cats*. That's enough to drive you catty.

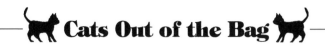
Cats Out of the Bag

111. Manx cats from the Isle of Man have three tail variations: rumpy or no tail; stumpy, from one to five inches long; and a full tail. One litter may produce kittens of each variation.

112. The term "raining cats and dogs" was coined from the days in seventh-century England when, because of poor drainage systems, heavy rains would drown cats and dogs and their bodies could be seen floating down the streets.

113. If a pair of cats can produce two litters of three kittens per year, how many cats will they and their offspring produce in 10 years? Over 80 million. Have your pets neutered.

114. Burmese cats may be traced back to a brown female, Wong Mau, who was probably carried into New Orleans by a sailor in 1930.

115. During the Vietnam War, the Army attempted to utilize cats on leashes to guide soldiers into the jungle at night. It didn't quite work as the felines made a habit of toying with the soldiers' pack straps and clawing on the G.I.'s boots.

116. Famed novelist Henry James wrote with a cat on his shoulder.

117. Cats have 60,000 hairs per square inch on their back and 120,000 hairs per square inch on their stomach. Pretty hairy thought.

118. It was reported that an Oklahoma cat, when given away to a California family, left his new family and 14 months and 1,400 miles later arrived back at his original home. That cat was OK.

Cats Out of the Bag

119. A Natchez, Mississippi, law prohibits cats from drinking beer. They'd probably hate Red Dog anyway.

120. At the back of a cat's foot is a single carpal pad that doesn't touch the ground. It apparently acts as a brake when the cat leaps forward.

121. The superstition about having bad luck if a black cat crosses your path grew from the belief that the cat was on its way to visit the devil.

122. The Sphynx cat is hairless except for some fuzz on the head and chest and is hot to the touch. He is sometimes called the moon cat.

123. Can you name the bad cat in Disney's *Cinderella*? How about Lucifer.

 **Cats Out of the Bag**

124. The English Nun's Rule from 1205 stated: "Ye shall not possess any beast, my dear sisters, except only a cat."

125. The male cat in *The Life and Adventures of a Cat*, an anonymous story published in 1760, was named Tom the Cat. It was after its publication that people started referring to all male cats as "toms." Prior to that time, they were called "ramcats."

126. Cat-scratch fever is an infection of the human lymph nodes and is not necessarily caused by a scratch. Cats don't catch the illness, they just carry it, and a human can be infected by just being close to the cat.

127. All outdoor cats have home ranges from one-half to 40 acres in length.

Cats Out of the Bag

128. Krazy Kat was one of the most popular comic strip cats of the early 1900s. Drawn by George Herriman, it could be found in the funny papers from 1910 to 1944. Krazy was constantly the target of a brick tossed by Ignatz Mouse.

129. Among the cat family, jaguars and leopards are superb tree climbers. Of course, the leopards are easiest to spot.

130. Art Carney won an Academy Award for *Harry and Tonto* (1974) as an elderly man who crosses the U.S. with his best friend, a cat named Tonto, thus preventing Harry from being a lone ranger.

131. Cleopatra's cat Charmain, who died after being bitten by an asp, was mummified. Guess I won't squeeze that Charmain.

# Cats Out of the Bag

132. One of the most widely known cats of all time was Puff. Puff, along with Spot, Dick and Jane, were subjects in the elementary reader, *We Look and See*.

133. Cats have a third eyelid, called the haw, which closes once they fall asleep. Thus, male cats have a he haw.

134. Over a three-hour period, a male and female cat may mate up to 16 times.

135. Susan Ford, daughter of President Gerald Ford, had a Siamese named Shan, who disliked all men except the President. The cat also got along with the President's dog.

136. About 14 percent of all cat deaths are the result of falls.

 **Cats Out of the Bag**

137. A study by the Animal Medical Center of New York looked at 132 cases of cats falling from two to 32 floors or "high-rise syndrome." Ninety percent of the cats lived and 32 percent did not require treatment. Cats falling from five to nine floors suffered the most severe injuries.

138. One British study of cat-preying activities led to a finding that about 20 million birds are killed annually in Britain by quick cats. Tweety-birds are exempt.

139. Thailand's good-luck cat, the rare Korat, was named by King Rama V. It is silver blue with bright green eyes.

140. Normal body temperature of a cat is between 100.5 to 102.5 degrees fahrenheit. That's no cool cat.

Cats Out of the Bag

141. According to legend, Dick Whittington, nicknamed Lord Cat and who was Lord Mayor of London three times between 1397 and 1417, made his fortune as a country boy when he shipped off to sea with his cat. After reaching a far away country overrun with rats but absent of cats, he rented out his pet and was richly repaid by the king of the country.

142. Pure-bred cats have been sold for as much as $3,000.

143. In Prokofiev's *Peter and the Wolf*, the cat is represented by the woodwind.

144. *Cats* debuted on Broadway in 1982 and became the third longest-running musical in Broadway history. The play is based on T.S. Eliot's *Old Possum's Book of Practical Cats*.

Cats Out of the Bag

145. Anne Frank discovered two cats living in her Amsterdam warehouse attic. She named them Tommy and Boche for the English and the German.

146. Three different stars played Catwoman, a foe of Batman and Robin in the 1960s *Batman* TV series. They were Lee Meriwether, Eartha Kitt and Julie Newmar. The latest Catwoman was Michelle Pfeiffer in the film *Batman Returns*.

147. The cat generally has 24 whiskers, 12 on each side of its face.

148. Top Cat was a cartoon cat whose TV show was roughly based on Phil Silver's *Sgt. Bilko*. Arnold Stang was the voice of T.C., a cool cat who lived in the alley of New York City's 13th police precinct.

 **Cats Out of the Bag**

149. While there are over 100 breeds of cats around the world, most of them are less than a hundred years old, and the Cat Fancier's Association recognizes only 37 breeds.

150. In North America, kittens between four and seven months old that are purebred and registered may compete in the Kitten Class in shows. Guess it's like kittengarden.

151. In 1966 actor Robert Loggia rented a furnished mansion in Beverly Hills at first sight. He had just won the starring role in the NBC-TV series *T.H.E. Cat*, about a cat burglar turned good guy. Once he took up residence in the house, Loggia found himself surrounded by images of cats in the fashion of cat paintings in the hallways, cat dishes in the kitchen and a huge cat carved of wood in the den.

152. A Cymric is the long-haired version of the Manx.

153. In 1939, Sydney, a ship's cat missed his boat in Bootle, and when the ship arrived 5,000 miles later at Buenos Aires, Sydney was waiting for them. It seems he caught a mail boat headed for the same port and made the trip six days faster.

154. If a cat does not learn hunting as a kitten, it will not grow up to become an efficient mouser. Aw, rats!

155. Adlai Stevenson, as governor of Illinois, once struck down cat legislation. The bill, an attempt to protect birds, would have required all cat owners to keep their cats on their own property.

156. What happens when cats and dogs get into a scruff? Eugene Field in his poem *The Duel* wrote:
The Gingham dog went "Bow-wow-wow!"
And the Calico cat replied "Mee-ow!"
The air was littered, an hour or so,
With bits of gingham and calico.

157. The cat, along with the dog, are the only true domestic carnivores.

158. Cats are like human babies in the fact that their eyes are very large in relation to their heads, which may explain part of our fondness for them.

159. While cats do have color receptors, they see most colors in varying shades of gray.

Cats Out of the Bag

160. Robert E. Lee was a cat lover, and during the Mexican-American War, he wrote and asked his daughter Mildred to send him a cat for company.

161. The Exotic Shorthair is similar to a Persian with medium-length hair and was created by crossing a Persian with an American Shorthair.

162. Cats shed more as days get longer, and while cleaning themselves they swallow hairs which form hairballs in the stomach. Feeding a cat oils or a bit of Vaseline will help remove the hairballs. And your cat won't squeak as much either.

163. Lazy cats have a retirement community named the Last Post, near Falls Village, Connecticut.

Cats Out of the Bag

164. In old Rome, feline feces was believed to have healing qualities.

165. All cats are digitigrade animals, which means they walk on their toes with the back of their foot raised.

166. The 1990 foreign film version of *Romeo and Juliet* starred 100 actual cats. Voices were furnished by Ben Kingsley, Maggie Smith, Vanessa Redgrave and Francesca Annis, among others. The only human in the film was John Hurt. Cat critics rate it at four meows.

167. Male cats are known as toms until they are neutered and become known as premiers. Female cats are known as queens. Around many houses, cats are known as the boss.

Cats Out of the Bag

168. In World War I, cats were used in submarines to detect foul odors and in trenches in France to warn of gas attacks. The cat nose knows.

169. Handling kittens for 20 minutes a day the first 30 days of their lives speeds development and increases their bond with humans.

170. Cardinal Richelieu had 13 pet cats and fed them chicken breasts daily. He hired Rubens and Van Dyck to paint portraits of his favorite, Perruque.

171. In 1280 the Sultan of Egypt and Syria left a will which provided a garden for homeless cats where they were to be fed and cared for. The garden was named Ghetel-Quoth or Orchard of Cats. It was freshly fertilized daily.

172. Huckleberry Hound shared a portion of his popular TV show with Jinks the cat, who was always after mice Pixie and Dixie, or as Jinks put it, "I hate those meeses to pieces."

173. Boston's Angell Memorial Animal Hospital is known as the Mayo Clinic of animal medical centers because of its many clinical records. It is also a center for studying feline leukemia.

174. Cats have rocked their way into numerous Top 10 songs over the years. Among them are *Cats in the Cradle*, No. 1 for Harry Chapin in 1974; *Alley Cat*, No. 7 for Bent Fabric in 1962; *Year of the Cat*, No. 8 for Al Stewart in 1977, *Honky Cat*, No. 8 for Elton John in 1972; and *What's New Pussycat*, No. 3 for Tom Jones in 1965.

175. Tigers have also fared well in song. *Eye of the Tiger* was No. 1 for Survivor in 1982; *Tiger* was No. 3 for Fabian in 1959; *I've Got a Tiger by the Tail* was No. 25 for Buck Owens in 1965; and *Tiger Rag* was a Top-10 hit for six different artists, including No. 1 for the Original Dixieland Jazz Band in 1918, No. 1 for the Mills Brothers in 1931 and No. 2 for Les Paul and Mary Ford in 1952.

176. And lest we forget, lions enjoy music too, especially *Wimoweh — The Lion Sleeps Tonight*. The tune was a No. 1 hit for the Tokens in 1961 and then was a No. 3 hit for Robert John in 1972.

177. The cat in the film *Breakfast at Tiffany's* was named Cat. Very original, Truman.

178. The saber-toothed tiger was not a tiger at all, but simply a great cat. Paleontologists refer to it as *Smilodon*.

179. "No matter how much cats fight, there always seem to be plenty of kittens." — Abraham Lincoln

180. The Bengal is a new breed that is a cross between domestic shorthairs and wild Asian Leopard Cats. This large spotted feline occasionally shows wild outbursts, a result of its lineage.

181. The average adult cat spends about 18 hours a day sleeping or catnapping, and it is believed that they dream. Do they call it human-napping?

Cats Out of the Bag

182. You can catch a glimpse of Cat Heaven in Walt Disney's *The Three Lives of Thomasina* from 1964 as a cat dies and visits a celestial catland.

183. Winnie the Pooh's feline pal was Tigger, who liked nothing better in the world than bouncing. Paul Winchell is the voice of Tigger in the Walt Disney cartoons.

184. St. Anthony is the patron saint of dogs and cats. The patroness of cats is St. Gertrude of Nivelles, while St. Agatha was also known as St. Gato (cat).

185. The lightest cat on record, weightwise, was Ebony-Eb-Honey Cat who weighed one pound and 12 ounces at nearly two years of age in 1984. He was an itty bitty kitty.

Cats Out of the Bag

186. The pussy willow is said to have gotten its name because of a crying cat whose kits were drowning in a river by a tree. The tree dropped its branches to help rescue the kittens and since then each spring, the drooping willow grows cat-fur-like buds in memory of the occasion.

187. All cats seem to purr at the same frequency of 25 vibrations per second. That's purrfect timing.

188. The cheetah has been timed at a top speed of 71 miles per hour. Talk about being on the fast track. Cheetahs have been trained to kill coyotes in the U.S.

189. In Japan there was a time when anyone who killed a cat was cursed with ill fortune for seven generations.

# Cats Out of the Bag

190. A cat named Wilberforce lived in the house at Number 10 Downing Street and went through four British prime ministers between 1973 and 1986. The official civil servant retired with a pension. What? No gold collar.

191. Domenico Scarlatti claimed that his cat Pulcinella helped compose his *Fugue in G minor*. He cleverly called it *The Cat Fugue*.

192. A cat's heart normally beats about 155 times per minute.

193. In 1996, Scarlet rescued her five kittens from a burning building in New York. Ignoring the heat and flames, she made five trips back into the building pulling her babies to safety. She suffered burns to her paws and her eyes were blistered.

Cats Out of the Bag

194. Daniel Boone had a pioneer cat, Bluegrass, that trekked Kentucky with him.

195. Cats belong to the class *Mammalia*, the order *Carnivora*, and the family *Felidae*. There are four Genera of cats: *Panthera, Felis, Lynx* and *Acinonyx*.

196. Cats have been known to become restless and eager to go outdoors prior to earthquakes.

197. The Chartreux is a wooly, blue cat with a large body and a tiny voice. They have been around since the 16th century and are noted for being quick to learn to come at the calling of their name.

198. The cat's skeleton is composed of about 250 bones.

Cats Out of the Bag

199. Many nautical terms were derived from feline fellowship — such as catboat, catrig, cathead, cat's paw and cat walk.

200. The Purina Cat Chow/CFA Invitational, held in St Louis in November of 1988, was the largest cat show ever in the U.S., with 814 cat show-offs.

201. In olde England it was believed that a sty in the eye would be cured if rubbed with a black cat's tail.

202. The first Siamese cat imported to the United States was Miss Pussy, a gift to President Rutherford B. Hayes in 1878. Renamed Siam by the first lady, she was a present from a member of the U.S. Consulate in Siam. Hmmm, the Kit and I.

203. Your cat got a tongue? Make sure it stays away from these plants which are just a few of the many that are poisonous to felines: azalea, caladium, chrysanthemum, elephant ear, ferns, morning glory, poinsettia, and rhododendren.

204. A Burmilla is a cross between a Burmese and a Chinchilla.

205. If your cat is non-pedigreed but still exceptional, consider the Household Pet competition of the Cat Fanciers' Association shows. It is for "random-bred or non-pedigreed cats" over eight months old, that are altered and not declawed. The cats are judged on "their uniqueness, pleasing appearance, unusual markings, and sweet dispositions, but are not discriminated against because of sex, coat length, age, or color.

206. June is Adopt-A-Cat month.

207. Japanese ships have long kept three-colored cats onboard for predicting storms and for guiding ships to safety.

208. Mark Twain loved cats. His four favorite felines were named Buffalo Bill, Apollinaris, Beelzebub and Blatherskit, but no Huckleberry.

209. The 1966 film *Born Free* was based on the true story of a lioness named Elsa who was reared by George and Joy Adamson, Kenyan game wardens. The film won Oscars for best original score and title song.

210. The Rex, a mutation, was first found on a farm in Bodmin Moor, Cornwall, England, in 1950. His name was Kallibunker.

 **Cats Out of the Bag**

211. Can you name four popular automobiles named after cool cats? Catch a ride in a Jaguar, Cougar, Lynx or a Bobcat. The first Jaguar rolled off the line in London in 1935.

212. Boots, a cat in Heber Springs, Arkansas, has a "fishing license" from the Arkansas Game and Fish Commission and has caught a 12-inch trout from the Little Red River. While Boots also hunts moles, she has no hunting license.

213. The cat is supposedly the only domesticated creature that can stare a human straight in the eye without flinching.

214. The whiskers of a cat, called vibrissae, are sensitive to slight changes in air pressure or movement and actually provide a guidance system while hunting in the nighttime.

Cats Out of the Bag

215. Cats and primates are the only species which can learn by observation. Kitty see, kitty do.

216. The Munchkin is an experimental breed of cat, shaped something like a Dachshund, as the result of natural mutation.

217. If you think that you are a cat, you suffer from galeanthropy.

218. Four signs of coming rain given by a cat:
   1 - puts his feet behind his crown;
   2 - quits frolicking and chasing his tail;
   3 - sneezes;
   4 - comes in the door dripping wet.

219. Teddy Roosevelt's White House cat, Slippers, was polydactyl (he had extra toes). Bully for Slippers.

Cats Out of the Bag

220. As a child, international singing sensation Jenny Lind loved to sing to her cat.

221. Cats were of great value in ancient China and Japan's silkworm industry as they protected the cocoons from rats.

222. A cat will bring some of its catches home to its owner, not as a present, but because the cat wants to teach the owner how to hunt and fend for himself. This is a mothering behavior.

223. The first book printed in English about cats was the 1570 satire *A marvelvos hystory intitulede, Beware the cat.*

224. Immediately after giving birth, a mother cat will accept and raise the young of other animals.

Cats Out of the Bag

225. Kittens double their birth weight in one week and by three weeks they weigh four times their weight at birth.

226. A game called "cat's cradle" was universally known in olden times. It involved the transferring of an intricately-wound string around the fingers to the fingers of another person.

227. The name of the cat belonging to Sabrina, the good witch in the *Archie* comic books, is Salem.

228. Want to watch two spooky cat flicks? Then check out producer Val Lewton's *Cat People* (1942) and *The Curse of the Cat People* (1944), unless you're a fraidy-cat.

229. The phrase "curiosity killed the cat" originated as "care killed the cat," referring to a cat's nine lives and that care will wear them out. Because a spiteful woman was also called a cat at this time and could be nosy or curious, came "curiosity killed the cat," referring to curious women.

230. The most famous tiger of commercial fame is probably Tony of Sugar Frosted Flakes fame. He's grrrreat! So is his voice, by Thurl Ravenscroft. Perhaps it was his popularity that caused Exxon to put a tiger in their tank.

231. "Thelma Lou, you're the cats." — Barney Fife

232. In Lemonine, Montana, a law requires cats to wear three bells to alert birds of their presence.

 **Cats Out of the Bag**

233. The first cat show in England was held in 1598 in Winchester at St. Giles Fair.

234. The Egyptian sun god Ra was known as the Great Cat. Rah! Rah!

235. While domestic cats are not mentioned in the Bible, lions are. Daniel survived his night in the lions' den, while Samson created one of the world's oldest riddles with "Out of the eater came something to eat, out of the strong came something sweet."

236. The phrase "a cat has nine lives" may come from early 1400s England when a popular recipe called for one part cat to nine parts chicken livers. That's what you call real cat food.

Cats Out of the Bag

237. The heaviest domestic cats are Down Under in Australia. Edward Bear weighed 48 pounds and Himmy reached 46 pounds, 15 and one-quarter ounces. Now those are fat cats!

238. As governor of California, Ronald Reagan signed a bill making it against the law to kick a cat in particular circumstances.

239. The Birman, or Sacred Cat of Burma, was believed by some to be reincarnated priests. These cats almost became extinct during World War II.

240. The great cartoonist Bob Clampett created two cartoon cats based on the characters of Abbott and Costello in the 1940s. Their names? Babbit and Castello.

241. Nurse Florence Nightingale had more than 60 Persian cats, each of them named for a famous man of her era.

242. One of Hollywood's coolest cats was Jackie the lion who used to ride to the studio in a taxi and eat at the commissary with famed director Cecil B. deMille. Jackie made more than 250 films including *King of the Jungle* with Buster Crabbe.

243. The American Shorthair has been around since "pre-Revolutionary times" in the U.S., and legend has it that it accompanied the Pilgrims on the *Mayflower* in 1620.

244. "God made the cat in order to give man the pleasure of petting the tiger." — Unknown

245. Siamese kittens are born with a white coat, which changes as they mature. The Siamese cats are known for being very vocal.

246. Mohammed, the religious leader, was a cat lover, and once, so he wouldn't wake a cat sleeping on him, cut the sleeve off his robe. The cat's name was Muezza, meaning "fairest and gentlest."

247. A cat's brain is very similar to that of a human being. Because of this, the cat's brain has been studied more than any other animal.

248. In some urban areas of the world with moderate climates, as many as 2,000 cats can inhabit one square mile. That must be inside the kitty limits.

Cats Out of the Bag

249. Referred to as "the cat with the patent leather coat and copper penny eyes," the Bombay is a cross between a Burmese and American Shorthaired.

250. You can have a cat on your auto license plate if you are from New Jersey. The catch is it appears with a dog. The plate reads "New Jersey - Animal Friendly."

251. According to tradition, tabbies got their name from the district of Attabiah in Baghdad. Jews there produced a fine black and white silk with a watered effect. When the silks were brought to Great Britain they were called tabbi silks. The likeness of the water marks on the silk to the stripes on the cat brought about its name of the tabbi.

252. In less than a second a cat can right itself from a fall.

253. Most owners of cats are couples, but with single folk, a larger percentage are female owners.

254. About 50 percent of cats get an hallucinatory high from eating, smelling or rubbing catnip. They have a specific gene which allows the catnip reaction, while those cats without the gene have no reaction. Maybe the other 50 percent are waiting to exhale.

255. In 1887 Harrison Weir founded the National Cat Club of England. Its motto was "Beauty lives by kindness." In 1898 The Cat Club was begun by Lady Marcus Beresford. By 1910, the various British cat clubs came together as the Governing Council of the Cat Fancy.

256. The cat from Charles Perrault's best-selling 16th-century tale *Le Chat Botté* (*Puss in Boots*) was a talkative creature and was one of three items (the other two were a mill and an ass) that a miller left his three sons. The one with the cat became a great and wealthy lord. There is a monument to Perrault in the shape of Puss in Boots at Jardin des Tuileries, Paris, France.

257. Figaro was the cat in Gepetto's workshop in the Disney cartoon *Pinocchio*.

258. The British government has an army of more than 10,000 felines which keep official buildings mice and rat free. What a rat race!

259. The clouded leopard has the longest canine teeth of any cat.

Cats Out of the Bag

260. In 1947 Paramount and Famous Studios released the cat and mouse cartoon team of Herman and Katnip. Katnip was the slick city mouse who always tricked the country bumpkin cat Herman.

261. Since cats are unable to lick their face, they lick their forelegs and rub them on their face. Hey, works for me.

262. The alternative pushing of a cat's front paws back and forth is called the milk tread. Kittens do it to stimulate the mother cat's milk flow, and often old cats do it when they are on something soft and warm.

263. A Florida cat, that had been left behind when its owners moved to California, later appeared at its owners' new home 2,500 miles away.

264. One of Walt Disney's biggest feline stars was Syn Cat who stole the show in *That Darn Cat* as D.C. and shared the screen with two dogs in *The Incredible Journey*.

265. According to some tales, people in parts of China used to tell time by a cat's eyes. On cloudy days, a vertical slit in the pupil meant it was around noontime, and the bigger the pupil dilated the later the hour.

266. Dusty, definitely a female, was a Texan tabby with the record for birthing the most kittens. Her last kitty, born in 1952, made her grand total of kits a cataclysmic 420.

267. To a sailor, a cat's paw is a light breeze that barely ripples the water, making a motion similar to when a cat pats water.

Cats Out of the Bag

268. In ancient Egypt cats were widely used as a defense against rodents and pests and helped to prevent famine and disease. They were deified by the Egyptians and a person could be put to death for killing a cat.

269. Cats are believed to recognize other cats by smell and not by sight.

270. The first Intercat (International Cat Film Festival) was held in New York in 1969 and organized by Pola Chapelle. The festival of cat flickers is to raise funds for those who feed stray cats.

271. A Chinchilla Persian cat named Solomon appeared in two James Bond films, *You Only Live Twice* and *Diamonds Are Forever*. The name's Cat, Sol Cat.

 **Cats Out of the Bag**

272. The cat's instinct for catching prey is unrelated to its hunger and it does not necessarily eat its catch.

273. Besides the domestic cat, cheetahs have also been tamed, and in the Middle East and India, they have been trained to hunt gazelle.

274. The first Himalayan kitten was Debutante, born in the United States in 1933 to cat breeder Virginia Cobb.

275. During World War II, Sir Winston Churchill had a cat named Jock that ate dinner with him and attended his meetings. He also had a cat named Nelson that hid under his bed during bombing raids. Another favorite was Mr. Cat who had his own place at Churchill's dinner table.

Cats Out of the Bag

276. A kitten is prepared to leave its mother after it is about three months old.

277. Eek! the Cat is America's favorite feline boy scout with his motto of "It never hurts to help." The Fox Network cartoon cat was named by his creator Savage Steve Holland, who has had three pet cats since moving to Hollywood: Ringworm, who jumped out a 16th-floor window; an unnamed kitten who was carried away by a hawk; and Eek, who ate some antifreeze and expired. Kum ba ya.

278. Care to visually snack on films about maneaters on the loose? Join Sabu in *Man-Eater of Kumaon* (1947), Ben Gazzara in *Maneater* (1973) or Tom Skerritt in *Maneaters Are Loose!* (1978). Humans provide the munchies.

Cats Out of the Bag

279. One of the most successful children's cat books of modern times is Dr. Seuss's *The Cat in the Hat*. Dr. Seuss was really Theodore Seuss Geisel. When the Cat made his first TV special in 1971, Allan Sherman spoke for the Cat.

280. In 1899, the American Cat Fancier's Association was founded, and the Beresford Cat Club in Chicago started the first American Stud Book on Cats and established the first American Cat Show Rules. It was definitely the year of the cat.

281. The first cats in America were rat-catchers brought from Europe on commercial vessels around 1620, while early French missionaries were believed to be responsible for introducing cats to Canada.

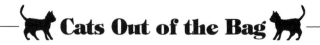

Cats Out of the Bag

282. One of the most valuable cats, a Singapura named Bull, was owned by Carl Mayes. He was offered 10 grand for Bull but said no deal (and that's no Bull).

283. Several cat calls are very similar to a human baby's cry.

284. The short-haired, brown-whiskered Havana Brown cat is a cross of the Siamese, Burmese and Russian Blues and gets its name because its color matches Havana cigars.

285. One of the largest legacies left to felines occurred in 1965 after the demise of Dr. William Grier in San Diego, California. The cat-loving doc left his two favorite felines, Brownie and Hellcat, $415,000.

Cats Out of the Bag

286. Grasshoppers make up half the diet of cats living on the Galapagos islands. No details on how high those cats can jump.

287. Egyptians trained their cats to fish as well as hunt and retrieve wild birds along the Nile River. Ever heard of a birdcat? No, but I saw a catfish once.

288. Romans were probably the first to introduce cats to Europe. The creature was a symbol of liberty in Rome.

289. The shaggy-coated Maine Coon cat is indigenous to the U.S. and has a tail like a raccoon. He is also the state cat of Maine. The first official Maine Coon was Captain Jenks of the Horse Marines in 1861.

Cats Out of the Bag

290. The cat and dog team of Ruff and Reddy was the first television cartoon series by the famous duo of animation Joseph Barbera and Bill Hanna, better known as Hanna-Barbera. *Ruff and Reddy* debuted in 1957 with Don Messick as the voice of Ruff, the cat.

291. Accidentally discovered on the set, Pepper the Cat caught filmmaker Mack Sennett's eye and went on to appear in dozens of silent films.

292. "You see a dog growls when it's angry, and wags its tail when it's pleased. Now I growl when I'm pleased and wag my tail when I'm angry." — The Cheshire Cat, 1865

293. Kittens can open their eyes about 10 to 14 days after birth and begin to hear about at two weeks of age.

Cats Out of the Bag

294. The biggest felines are the Siberian tigers who average almost 600 pounds with a height of three and a half feet and a length of 10 feet and four inches.

295. When a cat rubs you with the top of its forehead and nose, it is recognizing you as a member of its cat family. Either that or it has an itch.

296. When bringing a new cat or kitten into your home, the first place you should set it is in its litter box.

297. Probably the most traveled cat in history was a Siamese named Princess Truman Tai-Tai. A crew member for 16 years aboard the British ship *Sagamire*, it is estimated she covered over one and a half million miles.

Cats Out of the Bag

298. In a 1922 experiment, a cat was put in a sack and driven 4.6 miles away, then put in a room with an open window and left. Four-and-a-half hours later she was home.

299. Robert Mitchum, Tab Hunter and Alfalfa (Carl Switzer) hunt for a dangerous cougar in 1954's *Track of the Cat*. Amazingly, the cougar is never seen in the flick.

300. Grimalkin is another word for an old female cat or a malicious old woman. In Shakespeare's *MacBeth*, the first witch says "I come, Gray Malkin."

301. The tabby or tiger cat comes in four basic patterns — ticked, mackerel, spotted and blotched.

302. A cat at age 1 is like a 15-year old human, at 10 like a 56-year-old. The first three weeks of a kitten's life is equal to the first one-and-a-half years of a human. Talk about aging fast.

303. Of the cat's 30 teeth, some are for pulling and nipping, some for stabbing, and seven which cut like scissors for slicing. Or is that the Ronco Vege-matic.

304. "Letting the cat out of the bag" goes back to the 1700s when some farmers would put kittens in a bag and sell them, sight unseen, as piglets. When customers wanted to see the young pigs, the farmer would refuse under the guise that the pig might escape. But if the kitten began to mew or fight its way out, then the farmer had let the cat out of the bag.

Cats Out of the Bag

305. There are somewhere between 15 and 25 million stray cats in the U.S., and one band called The Stray Cats.

306. The Balinese began as offspring of purebred Siamese and are long-haired versions of the Siamese.

307. If a domesticated cat turns wild, it usually never becomes tame again.

308. The smallest feline species is the Rusty Spotted Cat from India with an average non-tail length of 15-17 inches and a body weight of three pounds.

309. A universal antidote for a poisoned cat is a potion of two parts powdered charcoal, one part milk of magnesia and one part tannic acid.

Cats Out of the Bag

310. The omnipresence of cats around the world is due mainly to the shipping industry's practice of carrying cats aboard ships to help control the rats.

311. A new mix of cat becomes a new breed only by official recognition by a cat association.

312. The 1959 Jimmy Stewart movie *Bell, Book and Candle* starred Pyewacket as the witch's cat for which the cat won the Patsy Award.

313. A kitten's only instinctive fear is of a large, hovering object.

314. Cats are "crepuscular", meaning they are active in early morning and evening. This is a reflection of their wild side of hunting at dusk and dawn.

 **Cats Out of the Bag**

315. The Cornish Rex and the Sphynx breeds of cats are less allergenic to humans. The Rex has no long guard hairs found on other cats and the Sphynx is nearly hairless.

316. Some studies show that male cats when neutered will add about three years to their lifespan.

317. The Japanese government declared all adult cats to be free in 1602 and made it illegal to buy or sell them.

318. Cats cannot live on a meatless diet. They must have taurine (an amino acid), animal fats and vitamins that only come in animal foods.

319. Kittens become fully coordinated at only five weeks old.

Cats Out of the Bag

320. There have been thousands of books written about cats. France leads the way in publishing feline literature with England second.

321. British Post Office cats began receiving a weekly salary in 1868 under the Cat System of "six or seven pence per cat - not enough to feed it adequately," so it would work to earn its keep catching rodents. In the 1930s, cats got a raise to a shilling per week. They got to get a better union.

322. The Egyptian Mau is one of the oldest breeds, going back to 1,400 B.C., and is the only natural domestic spotted cat breed.

323. Elizabeth Taylor was the cat on a hot tin roof in Tennessee Williams' famous play when it went to film.

Cats Out of the Bag

324. Chelsea Clinton's Socks was the nation's First Cat after a long line of Republicans. The last Democrat cat before Socks was Amy Carter's Misty Malarky Yin Yang. Socks, by the way, has an official fan club.

325. KATU-TV/Channel 2 in Portland, Oregon, has a gray tomcat named Bob as a weatherman. He wears sunglasses if he is predicting sunny weather. In cold weather, he wears a fur coat. But most of them time the feline prognosticator goes naked.

326. Zez Confrey wrote the jazz classic *Kitten on the Keys* and had a hit recording of it in 1921 and 1922.

327. "The trouble with a kitten is that it grows up to be a cat." — Ogden Nash

328. The town council of Piscataway, New Jersey, passed an ordinance requiring cat owners to prevent their cats from leaving their owners' property. The town is going to do what its name suggests.

329. *The Cat From Outer Space* (1978) was named Zunar J5/90 Doric 4-7 or Jake for short. Jake was played by siblings Amber and Rumpler. As for other spaced-out cats, the only survivor of the spacecraft Nostromo, other than Sigourney Weaver's character, in *Alien* was the cat, Jones.

330. The kitten seen meowing as a "sign-off" at the conclusion of *The Mary Tyler Moore Show*, *Newhart* and other MTM-TV productions was one of 10 kittens that auditioned for the job. That kitty turned its producers on with its smile.

331. Heathcliff is the only cat to star on his own metal lunchbox. Created by George Gately in 1973, the comic strip cat is a real terror to garbage cans. His TV voice was supplied by Mel Blanc.

332. Androcles was the Christian who befriended a lion by removing a thorn from its paw and later was spared before the Roman spectators when he and the lion met again.

333. Ragdolls are the biggest breed of domestic cats, with the males averaging 15 to 20 pounds.

334. A cat is not uncomfortable in heat until a temperature of 124 degrees is reached, however, its nose can feel changes within two degrees.

Cats Out of the Bag

335. Cats can hear frequencies up to 50,000 cycles per second, more than twice that of a human.

336. Some cats still milk on their mothers even while their kittens are nursing on them.

337. Domestic cats are born with two sets of vocal cords. It has been theorized that they meow and make cat calls with the true vocal cords or the voice box, while they make the purring sound with a false set of vocal cords.

338. There were three different Cat-Man heroes; one in a comic book and the other two in comic strips. The third and longest-lasting Cat-Man, in his own comic book drawn by Charles Quinlan from 1941 to 1946, had a female sidekick called The Kitten.

339. Perhaps the only 3-D cat flick was 1954's *Cat Women of the Moon* as U.S. astronauts play cat and mouse games with lunar cat women in black tights.

340. The cat does not chew. It swallows its food and relies upon its stomach's gastric juices to digest the food. These juices can break down bones, feathers and hair.

341. Along with cats, the fox, beaver, and rabbit all call their young kits.

342. When a housecat died in ancient Egypt, law required the members of the household to shave their eyebrows as a symbol of mourning.

343. The cheetah is the only cat that cannot retract its claws.

344. Cats are capable of three distinct types of sound: purring (mouth closed), meows (vowel sounds made with mouth open and closing) and hissing (mouth open in one position).

345. Tinker Toy, a male blue point Himilayan-Persian from Illinois, is the smallest cat on record. This cat is 2.75 inches tall and 7.5 inches long and that is no tall tail.

346. Judy Garland's voice was the star of the 1962 movie, *Gay Purr-ee,* as she spoke for Mewsette, a country girl cat who went in search of glamour and the bright lights of Paris. Robert Goulet was the voice of Mewsette's boyfriend, Juane-Tom.

Cats Out of the Bag

347. The Scottish fold cat's ears are bent forward and downward.

348. If you locate and pluck out the lone white hair of a black cat without being scratched, you will have a powerful good-luck charm. You also have a powerful mad cat.

349. Cats have special scent glands at their temples, on their face and at the root of the tail. When a cat rubs against humans, it is actually making its mark on them.

350. At one time, cats were used as good luck charms in new buildings. A cat's body would be placed between the walls during construction to provide protection against vermin. Good luck for who?

 **Cats Out of the Bag**

351. Rhubarb was a 14-pound alley cat that owned the Brooklyn baseball team in the 1951 film *Rhubarb*. Rhubarb later appeared in *Breakfast at Tiffany's*. He won several Patsy Awards for his work and was trained by Frank Inn, the man who won dozens of Patsys with his cats, dogs and pigs.

352. After a litter is about three to four weeks old, the mother will instinctively move them to another nest.

353. Seen in an actual newspaper ad: Free to good home - male and female tomcats.

354. Caroline Kennedy's cat Tom Kitten was the first Democrat cat to occupy the White House since Teddy Roosevelt's feline Slippers.

Cats Out of the Bag

355. The Turkish Angora is the only cat who carries its tail in a "full-time salute" over its back while moving.

356. The longest surviving fall made by a cat was from the 46th floor of a Manhattan apartment building by a feline named Leo on June 25, 1994. Forty-six floors down, still purring.

357. The cat's equivalent of a kiss is to touch nose to nose. Eskimo cats do it best.

358. In July of 1994, over a twelve-day period, Tabitha the cat flew more than 30,000 miles in a Boeing 747, after being lost in a 60 feet long and seven-inch high compartment. After her owner filed a suit to ground the plane, it took nine hours to find her, at which point she was flown home first class.

Cats Out of the Bag

359. For cat lovers who love to read, the Jean Baker Rose Memorial Library in Manasquan, New Jersey, has over 1,000 cat books on display. This is also the Cat Fanciers's Association's central office. The Cat Fanciers' Association, founded in 1906, is the largest cat registry in the world and has registered over one and a half million cats. During 1993 alone the CFA registered over 90,000 individual cat registrations and its affiliates produce over 400 shows a year showing over 100,000 cats.

360. The greatest hunter of man-hunters was Lieutenant Colonel Jim Corbett. He recounted his tales of tigers and leopards in India in his book *Man-Eaters of Kumaon*.

361. Americans spent $3.5 billion on cat food in 1994, more than we spend on baby food.

 **Cats Out of the Bag**

362. A cat's pupil can occupy almost all the eye or contract to a vertical slit so it can see in almost any light condition. The cat's field of vision is about 285 degrees, compared to 210 for a human.

363. Kittens feed solely upon their mother's milk for the first five weeks of life.

364. The California Spangled Cat, a cross between a Siamese and an Angora, was developed in 1971 to resemble a spotted wild cat and at one time was offered in a Neiman-Marcus catalogue.

365. The Turkish Angora, one of the oldest recognized breeds, was thought extinct until being rediscovered in 1962 at the Ankara Zoo.

Cats Out of the Bag

366. The metaphor "cat got your tongue" comes from the Saracens of the eleventh and twelfth centuries who punished those that blasphemed Allah by tearing their tongues from their mouths and feeding them to pets. Ouch.

367. Cats almost always meow at people but rarely at other cats.

368. A mob of angry Egyptians once killed a Roman soldier in Thebes for slaying a cat.

369. The long-haired cat in *Cat Ballou*, the comedy hit of 1965, was Jane Fonda.

370. According to *Rules of Thumb 2*, if your cat rubs your feet in the morning, it wants to stay in, if it rubs your face, it wants to go out.

Cats Out of the Bag

371. The feline star of TV's *Daktari* was Clarence. He starred in his own film, *Clarence, The Cross-Eyed Lion*, in 1965, several years before the TV series began.

372. ABC-TV's literate cat on Saturday mornings during the 1980s was named Cap'n O.G. Readmore. He encouraged kids to do just what his last name said.

373. Many cats are allergic to cow's milk; it ferments in the stomach and causes diarrhea.

374. In medieval England there were dozens of ways to "skin a cat" or to skin, dress and cook the cat. Good King Richard II condemned cat eating with a royal edict in 1384. Do not eat ye the cats.

375. The name of the cat behind the wheels in skits on *Saturday Night Live* is Toonces the driving cat.

376. Catgut is actually made from the entrails of sheep. And that's no bull.

377. During World War II, when the Allied forces entered Burma, the natives were unco-operative. After a British colonel had white cats stenciled on all the Army Jeeps and trucks, the Burmese people were so impressed by this image of good fortune that they agreed to help the Allies.

378. Disney turned to a talking cat in their 1986 TV movie *The Richest Cat in the World*, about a feline that inherits $5 million. Money talks!

Cats Out of the Bag

379. Cats produce about 15 different calls, which may be combined to make 25 different vocalizations. Call it cat chat.

380. Siamese kittens' eyes cross at about six to eight weeks.

381. A Himalayan cat is a Persian cat with the color pattern of the Siamese. If you see Himalayan, be quiet, it might be Himasleepin'.

382. The final execution of a cat for witchcraft in England was in 1712. It was about time they wised up.

383. It was during the mid-1700s that domestic cats were imported to America as black rats began to infest the colonies.

384. Disney and company borrowed Charles Dickens' tale *Oliver Twist* and came up with *Oliver and Company* in 1988, about a homeless kitten cared for by a pack of dogs. Joey Lawrence was the voice of Oliver.

385. Despite widespread belief, it is rare for male cats to devour their young kittens.

386. The American Wirehair started as a mutation in a litter of kittens born in 1966 in a barn in Verona, New York. This cat is unique in that every hair on it is crimped and springy, even its whiskers.

387. Edward Lear, author of the famous poem *The Owl and the Pussycat*, was fond of his very own cat named Foss.

388. The proper schedule of feeding kittens under six months old is three times a day, six to twelve month old should be fed twice daily, and any older than that, just once per day. Any food not eaten after a half hour should be removed.

389. The cat organ, a popular music box of the 1600s, actually included a live cat inside a wooden box. That was some cat a wailin'.

390. Tony Randall fell for a big cat in the 1965 film *Fluffy*. Talk about an odd couple.

391. The cat with tuberculosis may spread the disease to humans, though it is more likely that the cat caught the disease from a human.

# 🐈 Cats Out of the Bag 🐈

392. The Rex is also known as the poodle cat, because of its short, curly hair.

393. English poet Thomas Gray wrote his *Ode on the Death of a Favorite Cat* to Selima after she drowned in a tub of goldfish.

394. Jodie Foster and Johnny Whitaker run away with a pet lion in the 1972 Disney tale *Napoleon and Samantha*. It was Foster's feature film debut.

395. The study of the cat's uncanny ability to find its way back home is called psi-trailing.

396. Purebred cats generally live three months to a year less than mixed breeds.

Cats Out of the Bag

397. Cartoony Linus the Lion-hearted made his debut on a box of Crispy Critters cereal. When he became a Saturday morning star, Sheldon Leonard did his talking.

398. Besides sweat glands in their skin, cats also have them in their footpads.

399. Lippy the Lion was Hanna-Barbera's con artist lion whose sidekick was Hardy Har Har the hyena.

400. Billed as "the Smartest Cat in the World" is Princess Kitty, who pens a national "Princess Kitty says" advice column as well as her own club newsletter, *Pawprints*: "All the mews that's fit to print." P.K. can perform over 70 tricks and is the first cat honoree of a national fan club.

401. "A home without a cat, and a well-fed, well-petted, and properly revered cat, may be a perfect home, perhaps, but how can it prove its title?" — Mark Twain

Cats Out of the Bag

Cats in Cartoons

The Cat in the Hat
The Cattanooga Cats
Eek!
Felix the Cat
Garfield
Heathcliff
Jinks
Josie and the Pussycats
Katnip
King Leonardo

Linus, the Lion-Hearted
Lippy the Lion
The Pink Panther
Punkin' Puss
Ruff (of Ruff and Reddy)
Sylvester
Tigger
Tom (of Tom and Jerry)
Tony the Tiger
Top Cat

Cats Out of the Bag

Cats in Hollywood

The Adventures of Chatran, 1987
The Aristocats, 1970
Born Free, 1966
The Cat From Outer Space, 1978
Clarence, The Cross-Eyed Lion, 1965
Harry and Tonto, 1974
Napoleon and Samantha, 1973
Oliver and Company, 1988
Rhubarb, 1951
That Darn Cat, 1965
The Three Lives of Thomasina, 1964

Cats Out of the Bag

Cats on the World Wide Web

There are hundreds of cat-related sites available for your browsing enjoyment. Here are a few to get you started (these addresses are preceded by "http://"):

www.fanciers.com

    Cat Fanciers homepage

www.cfainc.org/cfa/

    The Cat Fanciers Association homepage

www.islandnet.com/~jensal/cats.html

    Pictures of people's cats

netvet.wustl.edu/cats.htm

    General information

www.covesoft.com/tca/

    The Traditional Cat Association homepage

www.cpi.com/cpihtml/homepages/edwards/toxic_plants.html

    List of common plants toxic to cats

Cats Out of the Bag

Cat Clubs and Registries

The American Cat Association
8101 Katherine Avenue
Panorama City, CA 91402
(818) 781-5656
(818) 781-5340 Fax

American Cat Fancier's Association
P.O. Box 203
Point Lookout, MO 65726
(417) 334-5430
(417) 334-5540 Fax

 **Cats Out of the Bag**

Canadian Cat Association
220 Advance Blvd., Suite 101
Brampton, ON L6T 4J5
Canada
(905) 459-1481
(905) 459-4023 Fax

The Cat Fancier's Association, Inc.
1805 Atlantic Avenue
P.O. Box 1005
Manasquan, NJ 08736
(908) 528-9797
(908) 528-7391 Fax

The International Cat Association
P.O. Box 2684
Harlingen, TX 78551
(210) 428-8046
(210) 428-8047 Fax

Cats Out of the Bag

Cat Magazines and Newsletters

CATS Magazine is a monthly magazine that has served cat lovers for over fifty years. Published by PJS Publications, Inc.; P.O. Box 420236, Palm Coast, FL 32142; (800) 829-9125. Cost $21.97/year.

CFA Almanac is published monthly by the Cat Fancier's Association, Inc.; 1805 Atlantic Ave., P.O. Box 1005, Manasquan, NJ 08736; (908) 528-9797. Cost $25.00/year.

Cats Out of the Bag

TICA Trend is published bi-monthly by the International Cat Association; P.O. Box 2684, Harlingen, TX 78551; (210) 428-8046. Cost $16.00/year.

CATNIP is a monthly newsletter published by Tufts University of Veterinary Medicine; P.O. Box 420235, Palm Coast, FL 32142-0235, (800) 829-0926. Cost $30/year.

Cats Out of the Bag

Perspective on Cats is a quarterly newsletter published by the Cornell University Feline Health Center; T 7018 Vet Research Tower, Ithaca, NY 14853, (607) 253-3414, (607) 253-3414 Fax. Cost $20/year.

Chats Canada is a quarterly newsletter published by the Canadian Cat Association; 220 Advance Blvd., Suite 101, Brampton, ON L65 4J5, (905) 459-1481. Cost $32.10/year individual or $37.45/year family.

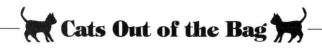
Cats Out of the Bag

ACFA Bulletin is a bi-monthly publication of the American Cat Fancier's Association; P.O. Box 203, Point Lookout, MO 65726; (410) 850-0574. Cost $30.00/year.

CAT-sumers Report is a bi-monthly publication by Good Communications; P.O. Box 10069, Austin, TX 78766; (800) 968-1738. Cost $18.00/year.

Cats Out of the Bag

Selected Bibliography

The ABC's of Cat Trivia, Rod L. Evans and Irwin M. Berent, St. Martin's Press, 1996

All About Himalayan Cats, Joan McDonald Brearley, TFH Publications, 1976

American Medical Association Encyclopedia of Medicine, Random House, 1989

The Animal's Who's Who, Ruthven Tremain, Charles Scribner's Sons, 1982

The Basic Book of the Cat, William H.A. Carr, Charles Scribner's Sons, 1963

Cats Out of the Bag

Caring for Your Sick Cat, Carol Himsel
    Daly, D.V.M., Barron's, 1994

The Cat, Muriel Beadle, Simon and
    Schuster, 1977

Cat Breeding and Showing, Meredith
    Wilson, A.S. Barnes & Co., 1972

Cat Catalog, edited by Judy Fireman,
    Greenwich House, 1976

Cat Catalogue - The Ultimate Cat Book,
    Judy Fireman, Workman Publishing
    Company, Inc., 1986

Cat Compendium, Ann Currah, Meredith
    Press, 1969

Catlore, Desmond Morris, Crown
    Publisher, 1987

🐈 Cats Out of the Bag 🐈

The Cat and Man, Grithe, G.P. Putnam's
Sons, 1974

The Cat Name Companion, Mark Bryant,
Carol Publishing Group Edition, 1995

Cat Tales, Robin Upward, Viking Studio
Books, 1989

The Cat's Pajamas, Tad Tuleja, Fawcett
Columbine, 1987

Catwatching, Desmond Morris, Crown
Publisher, 1986

The Complete Cat Book, Richard H.
Gebhart, Howell Book House, 1991

The Disney Films, Leonard Maltin,
Crown, 1984

The Encyclopedia of American Comics,
Ron Goulart, Facts on File, 1990

Cats Out of the Bag

The Encyclopedia of Animated Cartoons, Jeff Lenburg, Facts on File, 1992

Encyclopedia of the Cat, Crescent Books, 1979

The First Pet History of the World, David Comfort, Fireside, 1994

Good Housekeeping, July, 1993

Great Cats, J.C. Suares, Bantam Books, 1981

The Guinness Book of Records, Peter Matthews, Bantam Books, 1995

Leonard Maltin's TV Movies and Video Guide, Plume, 1996

Life, History and Magic of the Cat, Fernand Mery, Grossett & Dunlap

Cats Out of the Bag

Living With Cats, Gale B. Nemac, William Morrow, 1993

The Love of Baby Animals, Robert Burton, Octopus Books, 1976

More Strange Powers of Pets, Brad Steiger and Sherry Hansen Steiger, Donald I. Fine, Inc., 1994

The Name of the Cat, Barbara Holland, Dodd, Mead and Co., 1988

Name That Cat, Doug Cassidy, Crown Publishers, 1992

Newsweek, Feb. 21, 1994

The Observer's Book of Cats, Grace Pond, Frederick Warne, 1977

People's Almanac #2, David Wallechinsky & Irving Wallace, Bantam Books, 1978

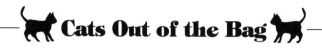

Cats Out of the Bag

The Quintessential Cat, Roberta Altman,
 Macmillan, 1994

Raising Your Cat, Rosanne Amberson,
 Bonanza Books, 1969

Rules of Thumb 2, Tom Parker,
 Houghton Mifflin Company, 1987

The Secret Life of Cats, Robert De
 Laroche and Jean-Michel Labat,
 Barron's, 1995

The Tennessean, various issues

That's Cats!, Grace McHattie, David and
 Charles, 1991

The Tiger in the House, Carl Van
 Vechten, Alfred A. Knopf, Inc. 1920

Time, July 3, 1989

*Understanding and Training Your Cat or
 Kitten*, H. Ellen Whiteley, D.V.M.,
 Crown Trade Paperbacks, 1994

Cats Out of the Bag

Understanding Your Cat, Dr. Michael W. Fox, St. Martin's Press, 1992

The World of Cats, John Montgomery, Paul Hamlyn Ltd., 1967.

You and Your Cat, David Taylor, Alfred Knopf, 1991

Premium gift books from PREMIUM PRESS AMERICA include:

I'LL BE DOGGONE
CATS OUT OF THE BAG

STOCK CAR TRIVIA
STOCK CAR GAMES
STOCK CAR DRIVERS & TRACKS
STOCK CAR LEGENDS

GREAT AMERICAN CIVIL WAR
GREAT AMERICAN COUNTRY MUSIC
GREAT AMERICAN GOLF
GREAT AMERICAN OUTDOORS
GREAT AMERICAN STOCK CAR RACING

ANGELS EVERYWHERE
MIRACLES

ABSOLUTELY ALABAMA
AMAZING ARKANSAS
FABULOUS FLORIDA
GORGEOUS GEORGIA
SENSATIONAL SOUTH CAROLINA
TERRIFIC TENNESSEE
TREMENDOUS TEXAS
VINTAGE VIRGINIA

TITANIC TRIVIA
LEONARDO—TEEN IDOL

BILL DANCES FISHING TIPS
DREAM CATCHERS
STORY KEEPERS
MILLENNIUM MADNESS

PREMIUM PRESS AMERICA routinely updates existing titles and frequently adds new topics to its growing line of premium gift books. Books are distributed though gift and specialty shops, and bookstores nationwide. If, for any reason, books are not available in your area, please contact the local distributor listed above or contact the Publisher direct by calling 1-800-891-7323. To see our complete backlist and current books, you can visit our website at www.premiumpress.com. Thank you.

Great Reading.   Premium Gifts.